In the Beginning
Our Earliest Ancestors

A round 700,000 years ago, as the ice retreated north, a band of our remote human ancestors arrived on foot from mainland Europe. They foraged for berries, nuts and edible roots, hunted animals and birds and made tools from wooden sticks or by laboriously chipping flints. Traces of their stay include some of Britain's earliest stone tools - found close to Southwold in the cliffs at Pakefield.

The climate and vegetation of East Anglia at that time wouldn't have been very different from the woodlands and fens today - summers were rather warmer and winters rather milder – but the big contrast was in the wildlife. Our ancestors heard the roar of lions and the whooping of hyena. They might have seen a four-metre-tall mammoth crashing

1

through the woodland, or a hippo lazing on the riverbank. Many of these ancient animals are now extinct in Britain - giant beaver, giant deer, moose, gazelle, rhino, elephant and mammoth – and predators such as lion, spotted

2

hyena, wolf, bear and the spectacular sabre-toothed cat. But their fossils survive, some of which you can see in Southwold Museum.

1. *Flint axe over 500,000 years old. Southwold Museum*

2. *Mammoth tusk. Southwold Museum*

The land bridge to Europe was sunk by rising sea levels

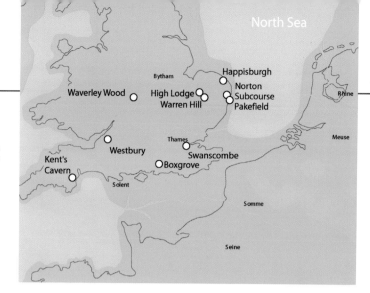

From Migrants to Settlers

At first, people walked here, over the land bridge that linked Europe to the British Isles, and along the banks of a river that vanished about 450,000 years ago. But these early visitors retreated south as the climate once again grew colder. Ice Ages came and went, and there were periods of up to 100,000 years when no humans lived in Britain. It was not until about 11,500 years ago that this country was permanently settled, but even then much of the population seems to have been nomadic, coming and going to mainland Europe. These migrations ended around 6,500 BC, when increasing temperatures melted the ice caps and the sea level rose - the land bridge to Europe disappeared and Britain became an island.

One of East Anglia's great advantages for the early settlers was its abundant supply of flints, which meant that people could hunt and farm with tools long before metal-working developed. It

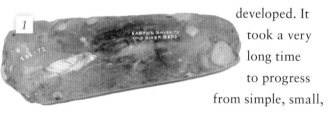

took a very long time to progress from simple, small, hand-held flints for scraping and cutting to sophisticated axes, arrowheads and spears. But this fundamental change enabled people to hunt more effectively, to cut down trees, to cultivate the land and provide themselves with clothes and shelter. Grimes Graves near Thetford in Norfolk was mined as a source of high-quality flints for tools, but not all such tools were locally made. People traded in flints over a very wide area – the Museum displays a particularly fine axe head (discovered at Easton Bavents) that came originally from Levallois in France.

There is little local evidence of the transition from flint to metal. Easton Bavents (most of which is now under the sea) seems to have been continuously occupied from the Neolithic to the Iron Age, and several Bronze Age sites dating from about 2000 BC are known farther inland - ring ditches and barrows at ancient burial sites. But there are virtually no surviving sites from the Iron Age, and the only signs of settlement have been a few isolated coins. Three poignant artefacts from the Bronze Age - a tiny flint arrow head embedded in a vertebra, the rib of an ox engraved with the image of a deer, and a bronze axe head found in a garden in Southwold – can be seen at the Museum.

Invaders from the Sea

About 3000 years ago people began to arrive at Southwold by boat. Some were settlers and traders - such as the so-called 'Beaker People', whose pottery has been found near Southwold - but others were raiders or conquerors.

The Romans came with an army in 43 AD, but left few tangible remains along this marshy coast, despite centuries of occupation – a couple of small villages at Knodishall and Wenhaston, some salt pans on the Blyth estuary, a possible signal station at Blythburgh and the occasional coin. But significant Roman finds, elsewhere in Suffolk and Norfolk, suggest a much more extensive civilisation than the local evidence indicates.

After the last of the Romans departed, about 400 years later, there was a new wave of invaders from across the sea, including the Angles and Saxons, whose Kingdom of East Anglia bequeathed us the astonishing treasures of Sutton Hoo, near Woodbridge. And they left a more local legacy, for Southwold's name is Anglo Saxon in origin - Sudwold, meaning 'south wood'.

In the ninth and tenth centuries the coast seems to have been used as a base by Viking raiders. The Museum has on display two magnificent examples of side rudders

from Viking longboats, one trawled up from the sea and the other found on the beach. Remains of a boat from this era were found in Buss Creek at Southwold, and evidence of a Viking quay has been discovered nearby at Frostenden. Local names like Sagin, Hurr and Upcraft are believed to be Norse in origin.

Then came the Normans.

5

1. *Neolithic flint axe, found at Easton Bavents. Southwold Museum*

2. *Bronze age engraving of deer. Southwold Museum*

3. *Bronze age axe head. Southwold Museum*

4. *Flint arrowhead embedded in vertebra. Southwold Museum*

5. *Anglo Saxon rune carving on human leg bone. Southwold Museum*

Southwold Under the Normans
Domesday Book

The Norman Conquest of 1066 was followed twenty years later by the compilation of Domesday Book - a record of landholding and economic life in even the smallest settlements. This provides the first glimpse of Southwold and its neighbours, Reydon and Easton Bavents.

The poorest of these tiny settlements was Southwold, a small island with no natural resources other than fish, no rich religious houses and a thin, sandy, unproductive soil. Southwold was held by the Abbey of St Edmund at Bury and every year had to provide 25,000 herrings to feed the monks. The island supported thirteen men and their families, giving a total population of around 65. They owned four ploughs, one horse, four head of cattle, three pigs and thirty sheep. There was no mention of boats or fishermen – perhaps the herring were trapped in tidal fish weirs, two of which are noted.

Reydon (held by Ralph Baynard) had sufficient land under cultivation to support 53 men and their families, with woodland for their pigs. They owned fifteen ploughs, one horse, five oxen, thirty pigs, one hundred and ten sheep and fifteen goats. Reydon had two churches while Southwold had none.

Easton Bavents was a place in decline, presumably from coastal erosion. A few men and their pigs scratched a living. There had been salt pans, but now there were none.

From Hamlet to Town

Over the following century Southwold grew steadily in importance. In 1202 a small chapel was built and dedicated to the East Anglian saint - Edmund, King & Martyr - and in 1220 Southwold gained the right to hold a weekly market on Thursdays, and then an annual fair. We know that the place was linked to the rest of the world by a crossing over Buss Creek, for in 1236 the inhabitants of Southwold were ordered to repair 'Myghtes Brigge' – 'by reason of the fair held at the said town.' And Margery de Cressy, Lady of the Manor of Blythburgh and Walberswick, was instructed to keep a ferry on her side of the river, for the convenience of travellers crossing the river Blyth.

At this time the river flowed south, behind the shingle bank of Kings Holme, to exit at the port of Dunwich – then the largest town in Suffolk, on the southern arm of the bay. But coastal erosion and massive storms, from the middle of the thirteenth century, washed most of Dunwich into the sea, clogged its harbour and made a series of breaches in Kings Holme. The seamen of Southwold and Walberswick aided the work of nature, cutting new entrances to the harbour, ever further north. Eventually they were able to deny Dunwich its historic right to levy dues on ships entering the river, and to claim the haven as their own. The process took several centuries, but it was a decisive story of shifting fortunes.

The thirteenth century saw another important change, for in 1259 the Abbot of St Edmund ceded control of Southwold to Richard Clare, Earl of Gloucester - one of the most powerful barons of his day. Clare received permission to erect a castle on what is now called Skilman's Hill – but he died in 1262 and it seems probable that the castle was never completed.

More important, for the longer term, was his establishment of a manorial court, held annually on 6th December – the feast of St Nicholas, patron saint of fishermen.

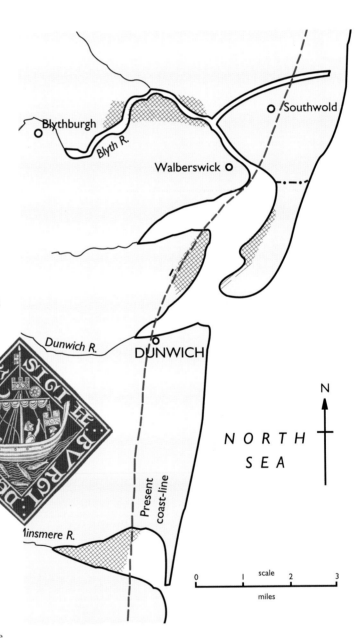

Map of probable coast line in 1066.

The Medieval Town
Pirates and Ale-Wives

Southwold was an unruly place, judging from the legal records. There were endless complaints to the Crown from their old rivals at Dunwich, as they lost control of the harbour. More serious was the petition of Lettice Eschot, in about 1287, who demanded redress against a gang of Southwold pirates, including a cleric, who had attacked two ships of hers in Orford harbour and made off with a cargo of wheat and herring, to the value of £700. That was an enormous sum of money, but the case dragged on, and there seemed little that anyone could do.

Records of the fourteenth century manorial court provide a vivid picture of these quarrelsome, sharp-witted townsfolk – often at odds with each other. They were fined for fighting, or infringing common grazing rights, or stealing planks from Mights Bridge – and for breaking the laws that governed the quality and price of bread and ale.

What eventually became the most important industry of Southwold has its disreputable origins at this time, for beer was the everyday drink of men, women and children, in an age when water was often polluted.

It was brewed by the infamous 'ale wives', of whom Joanna de Corby and Margaret Skilman were the most notorious. They appeared constantly before the court between 1345 and 1372, for selling ale in unmarked measures, at too high a price, or of poor quality, and Joanna's husband, Robert the baker, was in frequent trouble with the law, as were their hot-tempered servants. The 'ale conners', appointed to police the Assize of Ale, were themselves corrupt. In 1395 John Byeshop and John Candeler paid six pence each for failing to exercise their office, and in the following year were fined three shillings and dismissed. In 1456 forty-seven women brewers were convicted of breaking the Assize – at a time when the population of Southwold was probably less than a thousand.

1

2

3

Wealth from the Sea

It was the sea that enabled the place to prosper. Fishing was the anchor of the town's economy - local herring and cod from Iceland - and trade was of growing importance. Boats from Southwold shipped corn and malt, wool and hides, timber, butter and Suffolk cheese up and down the coast and across the sea to mainland Europe, and this was one of two ports on the east coast authorized to carry pilgrims, on their way to Santiago de Compostela. In 1434 John Waynflete gained a licence to export cheese to Holland and in 1451, together with Richard Skilman (descendant of the ale-wife Margaret) won permission to transport pilgrims to Spain – and at least five Southwold ships sailed the Santiago route over the next thirty years. Skilman was typical of this diverse economy. A rich merchant who gave his name to Skilman's Hill, he owned ships, traded overseas and may well have had a share in other businesses, possibly including shipbuilding, for which Southwold was becoming known. Some of those he dealt with had their own agents in the town, for the alien subsidy of 1485 records the presence of two Scots, two Flemings and nine men from Zealand.

The wealth that such activities brought to Southwold enabled the citizens to build a spectacular new church, to replace an earlier building that had burnt down. Its tower served as a beacon for ships at sea and the church itself expressed Southwold's civic pride. It seems even more remarkable when we consider that it was constructed in a sustained effort over thirty years, from 1430 to 1460, at a time of fierce civil strife – the Wars of the Roses. The only surviving trace of those wars is the small figure of Southwold Jack, dressed in fifteenth century armour, who originally served to strike the hours of the church clock. He reminds us of troubled times.

1. *A devil wheels the damned to hell, with a naked ale wife on his shoulders. Roof boss, Norwich Cathedral. Image courtesy Paul Hurst ARPS.*

2. *Southwold Church*

3. *'Jack o' the clock' - 15th century. Southwold Church*

1588 map of Southwold showing site of proposed new fort. National Archives

The Tudor Borough
William Godell and Southwold's Charter

The battle of Bosworth in 1485 brought the civil wars to the end, as Henry VII seized the crown. The new king made plain that he was determined to restore the threadbare state of the royal finances - so two of Southwold's most prominent merchants, William Godell and Robert Bishop, travelled to London, hoping to strike a bargain. A deal was agreed, doubtless reinforced by appropriate payments, whereby Godell was appointed victualler to England's anti-pirate fleet in the North Sea and made a member of the Company of Merchant Staplers (which had a virtual monopoly of England's wool exports). A few years later, in 1490, Henry VII granted Southwold its Charter as a 'free burgh', answerable only to the Crown. Godell and Bishop were appointed the first Bailiffs.

The Charter made Southwold independent of all local authorities. Governed by its Bailiffs (chosen by a council of prominent townsmen) the borough had the right to hold its own courts, set its own regulations, build a gaol, levy dues on ships and take a half share in the salvage

of wrecks. Two fairs were authorised - one on Trinity Monday and the other on the feast of St Bartholomew - and two weekly markets, on Monday and Thursday. It was a significant turning point for a place that numbered about a thousand inhabitants - crowded in rickety timber-framed buildings, surrounded by

sea, river and marshes - and it made one of them very rich, owner of ships and farms, trader in fish and salt and other commodities. When he made his will, in 1509, William Godell was duly grateful.

His first concern was spiritual salvation. Money was bequeathed to pay for his soul but most of his estate, once his widow expired, was left for the benefit of Southwold. Godell's bequest included almost all the land surrounding the town and sufficient cash to enable the Corporation to purchase a profitable farm at Walpole - an important source of revenue in succeeding centuries. Southwold Common and the Town Marshes survive as a memorial to our greatest benefactor.

The invention of English 'Bitter'

Southwold's Bailiffs instigated the custom of having the church bells rung to celebrate their election, on 6 December each year, and rewarded the bell-ringers with quantities of beer. This was no longer the soft English ale that most of their fellow countrymen still regarded as their national drink – but bitter beer, brewed with hops. East coast mariners had acquired a taste for bitter from the Dutch, their neighbours across the sea, and by the time that Southwold was granted its Charter, hops were being imported from Holland. But the real revolution came when the first hop fields were planted, a few miles inland from Southwold. By the mid sixteenth century William Bullein's Governance of Health referred to hops being grown in England: 'As by proof I know in many places in the countie of Suffolke, whereas they brew their beere with the hops that groweth upon their own grounds.' You could enjoy a flagon of Bitter in the taverns of Southwold long before most places in England.

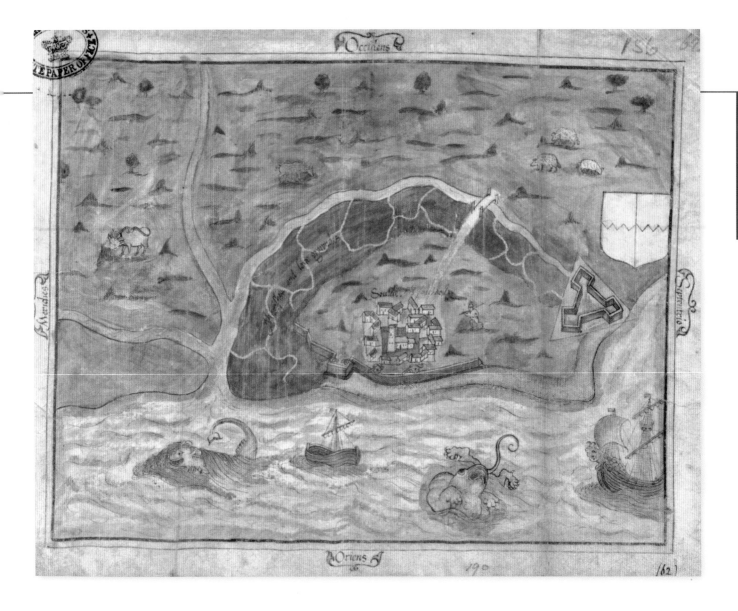

Fear of Spanish Invasion

The reign of Elizabeth I was a time of relative prosperity. A large fleet still sailed to Iceland for cod and ling, despite the falling demand for fish that accompanied the abandonment of the old religious fast days, and other maritime activities assumed increasing importance. Shipbuilding flourished and the merchants of Southwold traded in salt, cloth, malt, coal and timber - but pirates and foreigners were a constant fear. In 1588, the year of the Spanish Armada, the government considered reinforcing the town against possible invasion.

A map was produced showing the existing defences of a few guns on the cliff-top and the proposed new fort - but the Armada was defeated and the plan forgotten.

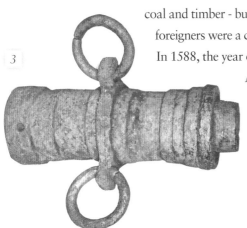

3

1. *Southwold Corporation seal 1490. Engraving from Gardner's 'Dunwich'*

2. *Henry VII, unknown artist. National Portrait Gallery*

3. *Breech of tudor cannon found in the cliffs at Gun Hill. Southwold Town Hall*

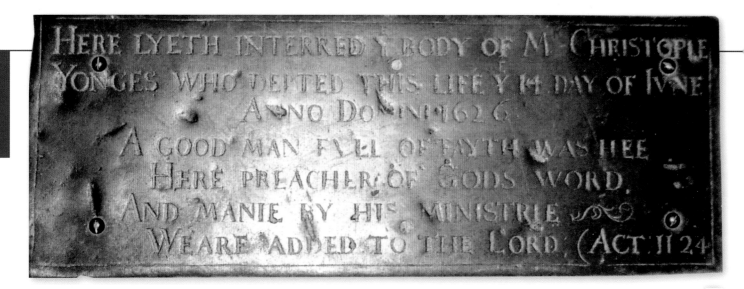

1

Tales of Woe
A Town in Decline

When Thomas Gentleman died at the age of 98 in 1609, after a long life as mariner, shipbuilder and frequently Bailiff of the town, the register recorded that he 'lived above fourscore years in perfect sight and memorie and in his flourishing time for building of shippes and many other commendable parts, he continued in his place unmatchable.' His death marked the end of an era - and a few years later his son Tobias published a gloomy pamphlet bemoaning the decline in England's herring fishery, in the face of increasing competition from the Dutch.

2

I   R

ENGLANDS WAY TO WIN WEALTH, AND TO IMploy Ships and *Marriners*.

Oble *Brittaines*, for as much as it hath pleafed the Almighty God to make vs a happy Nation, by bleffing and enriching this Noble Kingdome with the fweete
B   dew

Dozens of Southwold ships still sailed for Iceland every year, and the coastal trade continued to thrive, but both of these activities were hampered by what Tobias Gentleman described as Southwold's 'naughty harbour' and by the pirates who operated out of Dunkirk. A 'new cut' was dug in 1630 to bring the river mouth closer to the town, but even this improved entrance was frequently clogged with shingle, and the naval escorts that were supposed to protect the fishing fleets often failed to appear.

Economic woes were compounded by political and religious tensions. The epitaph of Christopher Yonges, a Southwold vicar who died in 1626, was a manifesto of puritan belief - with its emphasis on faith and preaching - but there was less and less room in the established church for those with radical views. The vicar's son (a preacher like his father) decided to seek a better life elsewhere. Denied permission to emigrate, John Yonges was smuggled aboard the Mary Anne and sailed with his family to New England. Three years later, in 1640, he founded the first English settlement on Long Island - and named it Southold.

Images defaced by Wiliam Dowsing.
Rood Screen, Southwold Church

Civil War

Such tensions came to a head with the outbreak of Civil War, in 1641, with roundheads and royalists fighting backwards and forwards across the country for nearly a decade. Southwold paid a monthly levy of £20 to support the Parliamentary cause, but it was not enough to protect the town from puritan intolerance. On 8 April 1643 William Dowsing arrived in Southwold with orders to remove every trace of 'superstitious images' from the churches of eastern England, and his handiwork can still be seen today, in the defaced images of angels and saints on the lovely rood screen. But superstition survived in the form of a 'witch bottle', discovered centuries later in the foundations of the Town Farm, which supposedly contained a spell, good or bad.

The execution of Charles I and his replacement by Cromwell as Lord Protector ended the civil strife but did not bring peace to the town – for England was soon at war with the Dutch. Southwold took on the burden of caring for the sick and wounded, landed from the fleet in Sole Bay, while its own mariners were pressed into naval service. In 1654 the Bailiffs John Godwin and William Wayneflete wrote to Cromwell's secretary, the poet John Milton, complaining that 'Southwold is at present destitute.

The town consisteth of about two thousand souls.

The causes of the decay of the town are the impairing of the harbour, the want of fishing and the charge of so many widows and fatherless, left upon them by several fights with the Hollanders.'

1. *Brass memorial plate to Rev. Christopher Yonges 1626. Under the pulpit, Southwold Church*

2. *Tobias Gentleman's pamphlet 1614.*

3. *17th century Bellarmine 'witch bottle'. Southwold Museum*

The Great Fire of Southwold

When a new entrance was dug to the cellars of the Swan Hotel, in 1989, a layer of blackened earth, smelling eerily of smoke, was discovered about a foot below ground level. It was evidence that had survived for over three centuries, of the greatest catastrophe ever to hit Southwold.

The Great Fire began in the morning of 25 April 1659, when a spark grew to a blaze, fanned by a wind off the sea, and spread rapidly from one timber-framed building to the next, roaring through the thatched roofs. Within four hours the Town Hall, Market Place, Market House, Gaol, granaries, fish houses, tackle houses, maltings, brew-houses and inns, together with 238 dwelling houses, were burnt to the ground. The damage was estimated at £40,000 and three hundred families were ruined, almost the entire property-owning population of Southwold. Collections were held as far afield as Yorkshire to relieve the town's distress.

Rebuilding began at once, but it took centuries for the population to regain its former size, or the town its prosperity.

By 1674 the Hearth Tax records show 153 habitations in Southwold of which 25 were empty and 66 too poor to pay tax. And the fire broke the continuity of Southwold's commercial life, as the old mercantile families were replaced by new names, often originating far from the town.

The landlord of the Old Swan, Goodman Wiggins, was one of those who lost his livelihood and disappeared from the records. The inn was rebuilt by John Rous and his son Robert, in time to provide refreshment for the bell-ringers and soldiers when the Bailiffs proclaimed the Restoration of King Charles II, in 1660. Later that year, on St. Nicholas Day, the Bailiff's 'coming in' feast was held once more at the Swan, as it had always been. Twenty-four sat down to dinner, for which Robert Rous charged 6 shillings per head, plus a further 25 shillings 'for wine and tobacco'. The total was nearly twice what Wiggins had been paid 'for the feast at Nicholas Day', under the dour regime of the Commonwealth, two years earlier. More significant, in the long term, was that the brew-house attached to the Old Swan was relocated at the back of the yard, as a fire precaution. The cellars of the present brewery date from this time.

BOROUGH OF SOUTHWOLD.

THIS STONE WAS ERECTED TO MARK THE TERCENTENARY OF THE GREAT FIRE OF SOUTHWOLD OF 25ᵀᴴ APRIL, 1659.   UNDER THE GREENS OF THE TOWN LIE THE SITES OF MANY HOUSES AND WORKSHOPS THEN DESTROYED. 25ᵀᴴ APRIL 1959.   WILLIAM J. BLYTHE, MAYOR.

The Battle of Sole Bay

In 1672 Southwold was headquarters for the English fleet under the command of the King's brother James Duke of York and the Earl of Sandwich, who are believed to have stayed at Sutherland House - one of the few dwellings to survive the Fire. At Whitsun that year the crews had been given shore leave in the town and most of them were still sleeping it off when the alarm was raised, early in the morning of 28 May. The Dutch fleet under De Ruyter was only two hours away – but it took the Bailiffs and a drummer boy four hours to clear the sailors out of the taverns and back onto their ships to do battle.

The English and Dutch fleets – perhaps 150 ships and tens of thousands of men – fought it out for most of the day, while the French (supposedly our allies) sailed away from the battle.

The Duke of York had to transfer ship twice, as Prince Royal and St Michael were taken out of action - and Lord Sandwich's flagship, HMS Royal James, was set on fire. Sandwich insisted on staying on board to the very end, and was drowned when at last he abandoned ship. His body was washed ashore further down the coast and was only recognisable by the Star and Garter on his blue satin coat.

The thunder of guns brought people hurrying from nearby villages to crowd along the cliffs, but there was little to see of the distant battle except clouds of billowing smoke. It ended inconclusively at sunset. The Dutch sailed home, but the English flagship was sunk and both fleets suffered considerable damage. About 2000 men were killed on each side and the people of Southwold had to care for 800 sick and wounded crewmen. For weeks afterwards the town Chamberlain recorded payments of a shilling to anyone who found and buried the body of a drowned sailor, washed up on the shore.

1. *Fire Commemoration plaque. Southwold Town Hall*

2. *In 1676 Phillipa Bedingfield married Sir John Rous, whose family rebuilt the Swan after the fire. Swan Hotel, Southwold*

3. *Cannonballs from Battle of Sole Bay. Southwold Museum*

Salt, Dissent, and Beer
The Southwold Salt Works

The chief business of the Town is for Sea affairs, for which purpose they are furnished with about twenty or thirty Sayl of small Vessels. The chief trade is to Iceland and the North-sea for Codd; they also have a Coal-trade, and a great passage trade to London with cheeses and butter; they have also something to do in Ship-building, and refining of salt.'

1

ESTABLISHED 1660

TRADE E S MARK

THE CELEBRATED SOUTHWOLD CRYSTALIZED SEA SALT

Richard Blome's description of Southwold, a decade after the Fire, shows that there were less than half as many ships as at the beginning of the century, but the essential ingredients of Southwold's commercial life were little changed. The exception was the salt works. Salt had always been a vital commodity for the Iceland fishing fleet, to preserve the catch of cod, and the merchants of Southwold had traded in salt as far back as William Godell's day – but there is no evidence of it being made here since Norman times. So the foundation of Southwold's salt works in 1660, by charter of King Charles II, was an important boost to the local economy.

The technology was basic. At high spring tides seawater was allowed to flood into a creek off the River Blyth and left to evaporate and concentrate, after which the enriched brine was stored in a well. From the well, the brine was pumped over Ferry Road to the salt works, driven by a canvas-sailed wind pump, where it was blended with mined salt in what was known as the 'salt on salt' technique - to improve the quality of the end product.

2

In the early days, this rock salt had to be imported but in 1670 big deposits were found in Cheshire, which assured a more reliable and cheaper supply. The strengthened brine was then evaporated at varying temperatures in a succession of coal-fired iron pans, to produce crystalline salt of differing grain size – and sometimes they used ale to clarify the brew.

At the peak of its production, the Southwold salt works had more than 1000 tons of crude salt in stock. But it was mostly a labour-intensive, low-profit business and the Salt Tax, imposed in 1702, meant that only the coarsest salt for the fisheries (partially exempt from the tax) was in consistent local demand.

Merchants and Dissenters

A gilded copper weather vane, dated 1661 and bearing the initials TP and JW, is preserved in Southwold Museum. It comes from the old Market Cross, a lead-roofed building raised on pillars above sheltered stalls, where the 'petty' business of the borough was normally transacted. The Cross was rebuilt after the Fire, and the initials are those of Thomas Postle and John Wigg.

Postle was a merchant, grocer and draper who nine years earlier, in 1652, had minted his own farthing tokens, to use instead of coins when these were in short supply. Those tiny tokens were embossed on one side with his name, surrounding the arms of the Grocers Company (of which he was a member) and on the other with the word 'Southwold' and a heart. The heart suggests compassion for the cashless poor, which was the overt message when the Corporation issued its own halfpenny tokens in 1667, 'For the Poore's Advantage'. That sense of civic duty was typical of the religious dissenters who dominated life in Southwold towards the end of the seventeenth century. Postle himself refused the Oath of Supremacy (to the King as head of the church) when elected Bailiff in 1662, and was promptly removed from office. But he served as Bailiff twice more, in 1671 and 1690, and most of his fellow councillors shared his religious sympathies. Their attendance at communion was only to comply with the law for those holding civic office.

The dissenters even shared the church with the vicar, until they were evicted when a new minister was appointed - whereupon they took temporary refuge in a malt house near Reydon corner. A few years later the Catholic King James revoked the town charter and imposed a new Corporation - much to the townsfolk's fury - but the 'Glorious Revolution' of 1688, bringing William & Mary to the throne, was accompanied by greater tolerance. The following year Southwold granted the lease of a building on the town farm at Walpole to 'ye saints in and about Cookley', for use as an Independent chapel - and Jonathan Cockraine (relative of one of the Bailiffs) was appointed principal trustee of the first Dissenting place of worship in Southwold itself.

When Daniel Defoe visited the town on a Sunday in 1722, he went to the vast church and found twenty seven people at prayer, 'beside the parson and the clerk' – 'but the meeting house of the Dissenters was full to the very doors, having, as I guessed, from six to eight hundred people in it.'

1. *Trade Mark, Southwold Salt Works. Southwold Museum*

2. *19th century photograph of manual and wind-powered pumps for Southwold Salt Works, probably little changed since 17th century. Southwold Museum*

3. *Gilded copper weather vane from old Market Cross 1661. Southwold Museum*

4. *Southwold corporation half penny token 1667. Engraving from Gardner's 'Dunwich'*

Brewers and Maltsters

Most of the prominent names of Southwold, in the late seventeenth and early eighteenth centuries, were new to the town - incomers after the Fire. And most had a hand in the brewing of beer, for which Southwold began to be famous.

John Skipp arrived from Norfolk in 1664 and set himself up as brewer and maltster on the High Street. He raised a large family, occupied a fine house and had time to enjoy music - he kept a pair of virginals in his hall - but the business ceased at his death, in a pattern repeated for other short-lived breweries. Two families, Nunn and Thompson, proved exceptions to this rule. They dominated commercial and civic life for more than a hundred years - as merchants, ship-owners, farmers, maltsters and brewers - and often as Bailiffs. It was not until late in the eighteenth century that their rule was challenged by the

Robinsons (who traded in timber from the Baltic) and the Mays, who took charge of the salt works.

The first Thomas Nunn came from a family of Dissenters near Walpole. He arrived in Southwold in 1660, acquired a maltings and brewery at the White Lion in Back Street (now Victoria Street) and was Bailiff two years later. From his house in the Market Place – on the site of the present supermarket - he could survey the comings and goings of everyone else in the town, and

the records suggest that he had fingers in many pies. He and his descendants took an active part in civic life and a portrait of his grandson, another Thomas, hangs in Southwold Town Hall.

Nunn's great rival John Thompson was sworn in as Bailiff in 1694. Thompson traded as a merchant in various commodities but his main business was beer. His house on the High Street had passed from one brewer to another, since being built by Richard Buckenham in the previous century, and he owned a cluster of pubs, brew-houses and maltings in and around the town. The most important of these was the Swan, which was the centre of gossip and civic intrigue. It hosted the 'coming-in' feast of the

1. *Town Charter renewed by William and Mary 1688*

2. *Thomas Nunn, Brewer and Bailiff.*
    Southwold Town Hall

3. *The Town Bull. Swan Hotel, Southwold*

View of North side of Market Place, prior to 1819.

Bailiffs and Corporation, provided refreshment for the town Chamberlain - who used it as an office to pay his accounts - and welcomed whatever visitors found their way to Southwold.

One such was John Kirby, whose Suffolk Traveller (1735) mentions 'Southwold's excellent springs of good water, which may be one reason why their beer is so much esteemed.' Less complimentary was Parson Woodforde, who arrived with some friends in April 1766. His diary records that they 'supped, dined and slept at an indifferent Inn, but very civil landlord, the Old Swan'. Woodforde was hard to please - he spent five hours on Southwold beach, looking for curious pebbles, 'but could find none very curious.'

A Cure for the Bull and Smallpox

The 'petty business' of the town was supposed to be conducted in the upper room of the Market Cross, but the Chamberlain preferred to transact such matters within reach of a flagon of beer – the cure for all troubles. His accounts for 1709 show that hardly a day went by without a few shillings being spent at the Old Swan, as he and the Bailiffs settled civic affairs over pints of beer or sack (sweet sherry) and a pipe of tobacco. There were serious matters to discuss, for the Town Bull was sick. Anxiety was expressed in June and by the end of September matters were so grave, or the beer so strong, that the Chamberlain was reduced to incoherence - recording that three shillings and sixpence was 'spent about ye Bull when sick and drink.' The patriotic necessity of drinking the Queen's health provided an excellent excuse in November, over two pounds being spent in this manner during the month, and so it continued for the rest of the year, until the 'Town Tennent' came to pay his rent on Christmas eve, and there was cause for further celebration.

When humans were ill with the dreaded smallpox, Southwold took careful precautions. The suffering sick, young and old, were confined to the Pest House, tended by a nurse and guarded by 'watchers' – to prevent them escaping. One of such outbreak occurred in 1742, when William Milbourne was Overseer of the Pest House. Milbourne's mother was a Thompson and his daughter was married to a Nunn – you might say that beer was in his blood – and his accounts for the two months of the epidemic make interesting reading. A tenth of the total expenditure was on alcohol - over a thousand pints of small beer, twelve of strong, nine and a half pints of sherry and three pints of gin - most of which was consumed by the three women, two youths and seven children who actually fell sick of the pox and were a charge on the parish at this time. Only one woman and two children died from the combined effects of smallpox and alcohol, which says wonders for the robust constitution of Southwold's inhabitants, or the curative properties of its beer.

3

Barges on the Blyth Navigation c. 1800. Unknown artist, Southwold Museum

Sea and River
The Free British Fishery

Long shore fishermen at Southwold used shallow-draught boats, which they pulled straight up on the beach, but the deep-sea fishermen (with their valuable cargo of herring and cod) needed access to a good harbour. That was always a problem at Southwold, where the 'lousie creek' (in Defoe's words) required constant work to keep the river mouth open. And then there was the danger of pirates, taking a regular toll on commercial cargoes.

Southwold's defences against French privateers were strengthened in 1745 when the government provided six 18 pounders to replace the ancient cannon on Gun Hill - and in 1750 the town was chosen as the headquarters of the Free British Fishery, established by Act of Parliament. The object was to revive the nation's fishing industry and compete with the Dutch, our long-standing rivals for dominance of the European herring markets.
£500,000 was voted for the endeavour, equivalent to at least £50 million in modern money.

Wharves and warehouses, a net house, tan office, cooper's workshop and a row of cottages in Church Street were built for this new venture, and the entrance to Southwold's harbour was improved by the completion of two piers. Fifty large busses (broad-beamed herring boats) were constructed and fitted out, and the Southwold Salt Works vastly increased its production (the Fishery was exempted

1

from the salt tax) - making a fortune for its owner, John May. When Thomas Gardner, the Salt Tax officer, published his masterpiece of local history in 1754, it was

2

The Southwest Prospect of SOUTHWOLD

A. Black Shore	D. Guild Hall	To the Honble EDWd. VERNON Esq.	This Plate is Dedicated	H. Bay	MMM. Marshes
B. Warehouse	E. Market Hall	by his most humble Servant	Thos. Gardner	I. Net Poles	NNN. River
C. Net House	F. Fort			K. Salt Works	O. Tan Office Q. Salt Office
Church	G. Boat Houses			LLLL. Common	P. EASTON

dedicated to the Harbour Commissioners and financed by a long list of subscribers, headed by the 'His late Highness, Frederick Prince of Wales' - the first Governor of the Free British Fishery.

There was a short-lived boom (several of Southwold's pubs were first licensed at this time) – but the combination of the treacherous harbour, a succession of bad fishing seasons and general incompetence brought the enterprise to grief. At two o'clock in the afternoon of Tuesday 17 March 1772, the remnants of the Fishery's assets were put up for auction at the Old Swan Inn, fetching £6,391 - all that remained of the original investment. The unemployed fishermen turned to smuggling, and battles with the excise-men dramatically increased.

The Blyth Navigation

The Blyth Navigation, established by Parliament in 1757, was intended to make the river navigable as far as Halesworth by widening, dredging and putting in locks. Local landowners subscribed to this new company - since embankment of the Blyth turned tidal marshes into valuable grazing and provided easier access to markets, at much lower cost. By 1761 barges were able to transport goods up and down the river, and cargo could be trans-shipped at Southwold - where coastal vessels brought coal from Newcastle or loaded malt and grain for delivery as far as London. For about a century, until the coming of rail, the Navigation provided a commercial boost to the town, more important than the harvest of the sea.

3

1. *Silver medal commemorating the founding of the Free British Fishery 1750. Southwold Museum*

2. *Southwold in 1754, showing new buildings for the fishery. Engraving by Thomas Gardner, Southwold Museum*

3. *Southwold Harbour 1822. Engraving by William Daniel. Crown Hotel, Southwold*

South east view of Southwold from a drawing by J.B. Crowe for Robert Wake's 'Southwold and its Vicinity' 1839

Parties and Politics
A Genteel Resort

On 1st August 1822 James Maggs - schoolmaster, auctioneer, diarist and general busybody - wrote a puff for the local press to advertise the joys of Southwold. He praised the town's coastal situation, the purity of its 'cool and vivifying breezes', its facilities 'for cold or warm bathing' and its abundant supplies of 'meat, fish and vegetables of the best quality'. Others might query the charm of those cool breezes, or suggest that the burgesses were wrecking the town's finances, but Southwold was now a resort, 'daily filling with visitors.'

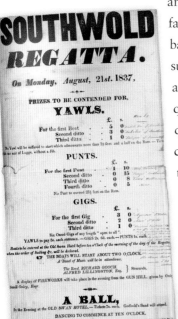

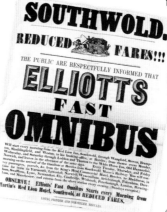

They came for the fresh sea air and to bathe - for their health, if not yet for pleasure - and the town did its best to look after them. The octagonal Casino was built on Gun Hill in 1801 - as a reading room for members - Thomas Bokenham made expensive improvements to the Swan and rival stagecoach services departed to towns as far distant as London. Annual horse races had recently started and 1835 saw the first Regatta, with races of the famous Southwold yawls - followed by fireworks and a ball in the evening, and a cricket match the following day. Even more evident, as a sign of the town's changing character, was the granting of building licences on Corporation land around Gun Hill, which enabled the gentry to construct large and elegant houses,

OLD SWAN INN, SOUTHWOLD.

T. BOKENHAM

RETURNS his most grateful acknowledgments to the NOBILITY, GENTRY, and COMMERCIAL GENTLEMEN frequenting the Town of SOUTHWOLD, and the Public in general, for the liberal encouragement he has received; and begs respectfully to inform them, that he has recently made such additions and improvements to the above old-established Inn, as enables him to accommodate Visitors for any period, with comfortable Beds, and Sitting-Rooms commanding extensive and pleasant views of the sea, and the adjacent country.

T. B. hopes, by an unremitting attention, and the select quality of his Wines and Liquors, all which he imports, to merit their future patronage.

An excellent Billiard Table and Bowling Green, commodious Stables and Coach Houses, near Post Chaises and careful Drivers.

Lodging engaged by applying at the above Inn, which is situated nearest the sea.

SLOMAN, Engraver and Printer, Yarmouth.

where they came with their families and servants for a few months each summer.

When a local newspaper listed 'the attendance of the nobility and gentry' at a Southwold ball, in August 1832,

the reporter emphasized that 'this attractive little Town still continues thronged with fashionable company.' No longer a place entirely dominated by fishermen, publicans, brewers and merchants, it had evolved the essential character of Southwold, as we know it today.

1. *Thomas Bokenham 'improved' Swan Hotel c.1820. Swan Hotel, Southwold*

2. *Gun Hill and the Cannons, engraving after watercolour by Henry Davy c.1828. Southwold Museum*

Municipal Reform

For most of the eighteenth century a small group of non-conformist merchants shared the duties and rewards of civic office without much dissension, and rents from the town property kept the accounts in surplus. But from 1799 onwards

there were increasing feuds, contested elections, accusations of corruption and mounting debt. Long established families like Thompson and Robinson were challenged by the newly rich Mays, who were accused by many of robbing the town coffers but themselves went bankrupt in 1814. The banker Solomon Grout (mortgagee of the town properties) then took charge, along with his friend the surgeon, John Sutherland. They undertook civic improvements - rebuilding the Town Hall near the Church and draining the marshes - but also engaged in several expensive lawsuits, defending ancient rights at crippling cost. Mortgage was added to mortgage until the corporation was more that £8000 in debt – with interest payments swallowing more than a third of annual income.

Following the Great Reform Act of 1832, a Royal Commission was appointed to examine the conduct of local government. The Municipal Commissioner who visited Southwold just before Christmas the following year was greeted by piles of petitions, libellous accusations and the evidence of shocking mismanagement: 'With an income of £1000 a year, [not] a single sixpence was spent for the benefit of the town.' As a result of his report, the Bailiffs and their colleagues were replaced by a Mayor, four aldermen and twelve councillors – but any hopes that the reformed Corporation would set new standards of probity were dashed from the start. At the meeting in 1835 to elect the first Mayor, seven votes were cast for each of two rival candidates, one of whom was a Dissenter (legally ineligible to hold municipal office) - the brewer and maltster William Crisp. As Chairman of the meeting, Crisp used his casting vote in his own favour.

The Mayor then decided that the existing Town Hall was insufficiently splendid for the reformed Borough, despite being rebuilt in 1815 – so the Corporation acquired a fine house next to the Swan, recently erected by Thomas Bokenham. Those who occupied the new Council Chamber did little to justify such self-importance. Within a generation quarrels and cronyism were rife, and the 'reformed' regime seemed no better than the old.

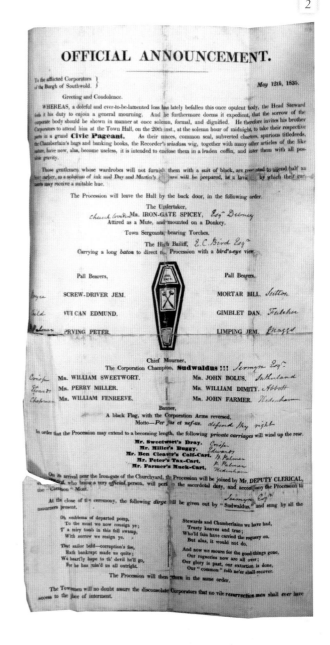

Trades Old and New
Ropes and Sails

Sail making and rope spinning had been practised in Southwold since the earliest times and continued to flourish in the nineteenth century. Sail-lofts filled the upper floors of several houses in East Street, and a sail-maker occupied the council chamber of the old Town Hall.

The walker or spinner had to walk backwards from the spinning wheel, paying out the hemp fibre from a large hank wound round his waist, as a boy turned the wheel.

Both Goodwin and Oldring had ceased trading by the end of the century but one of their employees, William Button, set up in business on his own account and invented an automatic wind-assisted device to turn the spinning wheel. When he died in 1935, aged 90, he was described as England's last hand rope maker.

Rope making, by contrast, took place in the open air, and there were at least three 'rope walks' in the town. One was Jasper Goodwin's, running from Spinners Lane to the marsh, across what was to become the railway track. The other two were centred on Henry Oldring's works in Cumberland Road. His short walk stretched to Field Stile Road while another, much longer, ran past the Church to North Green.

1. *William Crisp - Brewer, Maltser and first Mayor of Southwold. Adnams Archive*

2. *Lampoon on the death of the old corporation 1835. Southwold Museum*

3. *Rope spinning c. 1900. Southwold Museum*

The Black Mill, c 1880. Southwold Museum

Windmills on the Common

Another medieval trade, almost untouched by time, was flour milling – still carried on in creaking, dangerous windmills, dominating the horizon. Two such mills were visible on the Common when the Southwold artist Henry Davy drew a series of sketches of the town in October 1823.

One was an old post mill on the southernmost, windiest side - the Town Mill, also known as the White Mill – which had been operating since at least 1653. Its exposed position and rickety construction meant that it was often damaged by storms, losing its sails (as it did in 1738) or being blown over and then re-built, until its remains were finally cleared away in 1898. More sheltered, and much more solid, was the Great or Black Mill, which was transported here from Great Yarmouth and erected on the Common by Robert Dawson in 1798, on the site now occupied by St Barnabas residential home. In 1803 it was leased to Peregrine Edwards, with the Town paying for its upkeep on the understanding that Mr. Edwards would charge the poor just one shilling for every sack of corn he milled for them. Mill Lane and Black Mill Road recall this Mill's history.

The last windmill to be erected at Southwold was the New Mill, built in 1841 by the Vicar, Rev Rous Birch, on Church land at the corner of Field Stile and Cumberland Roads. His initiative was much disliked by the townsfolk, who saw it as an attack on the Dissenters who operated the other two mills. They responded with a scandalous rhyme. 'Who gives to angry passion vent, And built a mill to grind dissent, Showing thereby his mal-intent? Our Parson.' New Mill was ill fated from the start – it was damaged by storms and eventually, under the ownership of Mr. Baggott, burned down in its 35th year.

Windmills became redundant in 1894, when two young entrepreneurs, C.R. Smith and H.W. Girling, commissioned a modern, brick-built, roller mill on North Green.

1. *Ernest Adnams takes reins for annual brewery outing c. 1875. Adnams Archive*

2. *The first brew of Adnams Tally Ho, 1880. Adnams Archive*

Sole Bay Brewery 1866. Owner Samuel Hayden Fitch in top hat and white beard. Adnams Archive.

The Sole Bay Brewery

In 1825, burdened by debt, Thomas Bokenham sold off the brew-house at the back of the Old Swan inn, which he had acquired seven years earlier. It was bought for £350 by William Crisp, the maltster from Beccles who became Southwold's first Mayor. Crisp re-built and equipped the Sole Bay Brewery - as a distinct business, separate from the Swan

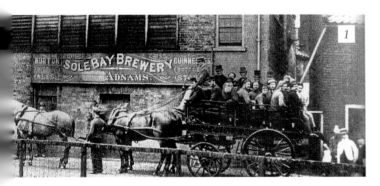

– and made it famous for the quality of its beer. By 1839 Robert Wake was able to claim that 'the home consumption of Malt, under the name of CRISPS ALE, is very considerable. This refreshing, if modestly used, beverage is universally

admired for the purity and delicious flavour imparted to it, no less for the unadulterated genuineness of its composition than the intrinsic purity of the water which enters into it.'

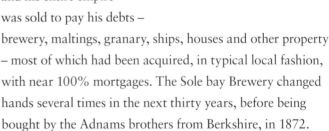

Crisp died in 1844 and his entire empire was sold to pay his debts – brewery, maltings, granary, ships, houses and other property – most of which had been acquired, in typical local fashion, with near 100% mortgages. The Sole bay Brewery changed hands several times in the next thirty years, before being bought by the Adnams brothers from Berkshire, in 1872.

George Adnams soon got bored with country life, departed

for Africa and was eaten by a crocodile, while his brother Ernest stayed in Southwold and formed a partnership with his brewer, Thomas Sargeant. To attract new capital, their partnership was converted to a Limited Company in 1890.

The inaugural meeting was held on 11 July but the minutes were almost certainly written several years later and are tersely uninformative. 'The Comptroller [Ernest Adnams] stated that this meeting was called in order to comply with the Act of Parliament. He reported that the business of the Company was prospering favourably.'

For a while that seemed to be true, as the Brewery was rebuilt, and expensive investments were made in pubs and hotels - but the business was overstretched. Within a decade, the Company was on the verge of insolvency.

1. *Southwold Town Pump 1873.*

2. *Employee check-in tokens for Child's ironworks. Southwold Museum*

3. *Child's official plate for Southwold Gas light Co, 1848. Southwold Museum*

4. *Gas Light by Child. Southwold Museum*

Southwold Church Gates 1838.

3

4

Iron and Gas

Southwold may never have produced an industrial entrepreneur on the scale of Garret of Leiston or Ransome of Ipswich - whose agricultural machinery was exported all over the world - but it did have its own family of iron-founders, with an unusual streak of invention.

2

Their name was Child, which is preserved in the name of Child's Yard, where Edmund Child established his workshop in the early 1800s, behind his house in the Market Place. Child made anything that his clients asked him for - including the iron coffin in which Miss Caroline Acton was interred near Ipswich in 1838 - but it was his son, George Edmund, who was the real inventor.

George Child was an exceptionally innovative engineer and draughtsman, who took charge of the family business in 1841. He is said to have designed some of England's earliest gasometers, including the 26ft diameter 'tank' that he constructed off Station Road, when he established the Southwold Gas Light Company in March 1848. By September that year the town had its own street lighting, with Child's gas piped to lamp standards made at the Child iron foundry – one of which survives at the entrance to the Museum. Other examples of his handiwork, dotted around the town, include the elaborate Church gates (1838), a sturdy water tank that now stands outside the Swan Hotel (1849), and the Town Pump in the marketplace (1873) – with its spout and finial decorations in the form of herrings.

Safety at Sea
The Beach Companies

In 1850, sixteen fishermen's families were living in poverty in wooden huts on Southwold beach, in danger from high tides, gales and cliff falls. Others more fortunate were members of the Beach Companies, which originated as informal gangs to help launch and land the fishing boats, but gradually concentrated on providing services to ships visiting the port. They operated large, shallow-draft yawls, powered by sail and oars, and smaller gigs, manned by rowers (often with shares held by local merchants) – and they made their living by piloting vessels, helping to load or unload cargo, ferrying passengers and salvaging wrecks - when saving lives reputedly took second place to scavenging cargo. On one occasion the crew of a yawl even managed to recapture a ship from the old enemy, as recorded by the coxswain, in 1814. 'Retoke a Collier Brig with Jubilee Pilot Boat, from a French luger - Put 5 Frenchmen on Shore at Southwold.' And sometimes there was a bit of smuggling, despite the presence of Excise men, on the lookout from the cliff top.

The Beach Companies took their names from different sections of the cliffs - North or Kilcock Cliff, Long Island, New York (going north to south) – and then there was California, the sandy beach opposite Ferry Road. Each Company had its own pilot-house or communal watch tower, on the lookout for ships in need of assistance. The New York Cliff House existed as early as 1760, close to Gun Hill, while the Long Island lookout was at the end of East Street, and the Kilcock near St James's Green. The origin of these American names is long forgotten, but the rivalry between the different Companies was still vivid in the memory of old men, as recently as the 1970s. Pitched battles were not uncommon.

The most notorious incident was in 1856, when two rival Beach Companies launched their yawls to aid a ship in the bay. As they raced to be first on the scene, the Kilcock's Swiftsure ran down the Long Island Reliance and sank her. Soon afterwards the Long Island men seized the Swiftsure and sold her to pay for repairs to the Reliance, which they had somehow recovered from the seabed. Nil Desperandum ('never despair') was the ironic name for Swiftsure's replacement, but she was always known as the Nelly, as was the pub where the Kilcock men preferred to drink, the Lord Nelson.

The Sailors Reading Room

One response to these lawless times was the foundation of the Southwold Lifeboat Society in 1840, manned by volunteer crews from all the Beach Companies. Another was the Southwold Sailors Reading Room - built in 1864 by the widow of a retired naval officer as a memorial to her husband, Captain Rayley. The late Captain had been a devout churchgoer and his widow hoped to persuade the local mariners to spend less time in the pubs, particularly on Sundays. So bible readings were organised, books and newspapers provided, tea was served and the demon drink strictly forbidden - but the Lord Nelson was almost next door, for those who felt in need of a pint. And gradually a collection of model boats was acquired, often made by the seamen whose photos now line the walls. The Reading Room today combines something of its original purpose with a display that serves as a treasured reminder of Southwold's maritime past.

1. *Southwold Beach c.1880. Southwold Museum.*

2. *Model of the beach punt 'Rapid'. Southwold Sailors' Reading Room*

The Southwold Lifeboats

When James Maggs looked out from the cliff top in 1843, he saw 'a fleet of from 7 to 8 hundred sail of vessels appearing between the two Nesses' - the promontories of Easton Ness and Dunwich. Sudden storms, shifting sandbanks and poor seamanship inevitably took their toll. Nineteenth century records list 283 shipwrecks in the bay,

The Museum displays two figureheads that recall those disasters. One is from the London registered barque Princess Augusta, which was stranded near the shore in 1838 and became a total wreck. The other, affectionately known as 'Lucilla', was washed up on the beach from a ship that probably traded in fruit and wine from the Mediterranean – judging by the bunch of grapes that she holds in one hand. She was carved around 1820. More figureheads are preserved in the Sailors Reading Room.

The foundation of the Southwold Lifeboat Society in 1840 meant that saving those in peril at sea was properly organised for the first time. Launched from the beach and powered by a combination of sail and oars, the early lifeboats had none of the safety systems of modern vessels, but made many heroic rescues in dangerous conditions – and the great coxes were legendary.

They included John Craigie, who served as a lifeboat-man for fifty years, and his successor as cox, Sam May, who himself served thirty years until retiring in 1918. Both came from local families of fishermen, with a knowledge of the North Sea in all weathers, and both were closely associated with Southwold's most famous lifeboat, which they helped design and skippered in turn for all of its working life.

This was the Alfred Corry, the last of the sailing lifeboats. A massively sturdy vessel, manned by a crew of eighteen, it was launched 41 times on service, between 1893 and 1918, saving 47 lives and winning numerous awards for its crew - including medals from the President of France and the Queen of the Netherlands. The Alfred Corry went though many changes of fortune after being de-commissioned, until it was eventually saved, returned to Southwold and magnificently restored. It is now preserved in its own Museum (formerly the lifeboat house at Cromer) near the mouth of the harbour. Close by stands the present Lifeboat Station, from which local crews still set forth in all weathers to save lives at sea.

Salvaging cargo from the wreck of the 'Augusta'.1838 Southwold Museum

The Lighthouse

In 1887 it was decided that Southwold needed a lighthouse, to reduce the number of wrecks in Sole Bay. A temporary wooden structure was built on California sands, while a permanent site was prepared in the town itself, near the coastguard station.

In a huge logistical exercise, the goods waggons of the local coal merchant, Thomas Moy & Co, were pressed into use on the newly built Southwold Railway, transporting the million and half bricks that were needed to build the tower.

The mayor, Mr. Eustace Grubbe, laid the first brick in May 1889, and ten months later it was time to install the lantern - which arrived from Harwich in two sections on Moy's wagons. The light was inaugurated by Trinity House on 3 September 1890.

Southwold Lighthouse was electrified and de-manned in 1938 – and has recently been re-equipped with an even more powerful lamp, to compensate for the decommissioning of the Orford Light, abandoned to erosion by the sea. The beacon flashes four times every twenty seconds, showing red at the sides as a warning of dangerous shoals to north and south, and white from a distance, for navigation.

1. *'Lucilla' and 'Princess Augusta' figureheads. Southwold Museum*

2. *Sam May, lifeboat coxwain c.1890 Southwold Museum*

3. *Restoring the 'Alfred Corry'. Alfred Corry Museum*

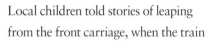

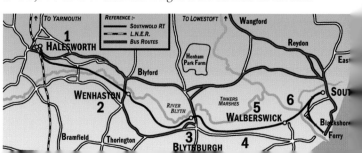
SOUTHWOLD RAILWAY GALA.
OPENING DAY
WEDNESDAY, SEPT. 24TH, 1879.
HORSE & FOOT
RACES
WITH OTHER SPORTS.
FIREWORKS AND GENERAL ILLUMINATION
SPECIAL TRAINS.

The Age of Steam
The Southwold Railway

The railway mania of the 1840s and 50s saw a network of lines criss-crossing Norfolk and Suffolk, promoted by entrepreneurs such as Morton Peto, the driving force behind the development of Lowestoft. By 1859, the East Suffolk Railway provided direct services from Lowestoft to London and there was increasing pressure to connect Southwold to the network. After much public discussion and many delays a group of businessmen formed the Southwold Railway Company, with a capital of £53,000, and Parliament authorised the new line in 1876. The railway linking Southwold to Halesworth opened three years later, in 1879.

It was built on the cheap on a three foot gauge - unique in England - with a speed restriction of 16 mph that allowed it to economise on signal systems, despite the fact that the route had

easy gradients and the only major civil engineering work was the swing bridge over the River Blyth. There is also a local legend that the rolling stock for the Southwold Railway was a cancelled export order for the Chinese Empress - a supposition hotly denied by railway historians but typical of the myths surrounding this entire venture.

Local children told stories of leaping from the front carriage, when the train slowed for a bend, and jumping on again, having picked a bunch of daffodils – or of tossing out bundles of newspapers to farms along the way. Sometimes passengers had to assist the guard to chase cattle off the line, or wait while the driver stopped for a late-

running regular. Frost could cause the wheels to slip as the train climbed the slope to Halesworth, whereupon horses would be hitched to the engine for the last few yards

of the journey. Straw was strewn on the third class carriage floors in winter, while first class passengers were given foot warmers. And the many minor mishaps provided Southwold's favourite cartoonist, Reg Carter, with a wealth of entertaining material.

Despite this air of eccentricity, the Southwold Railway was initially successful. The beauty of the route along the Blyth estuary and the convenience of the line for freight generated plenty of business, if not much profit. 65,000 passengers and 5,000 tons of assorted freight were carried in the first

Model of Southwold Belle paddle steamer.
Sailors' Reading Room

year, rising to a peak of 108,600 and 13,800 respectively by 1913. The following year a long-planned spur was opened to Southwold Harbour - just as war broke out and the fishing industry collapsed. It was the beginning of a slow decline.

By the 1920s the rolling stock and equipment were old and worn, the speed restriction and need to transfer the goods between different gauges were commercial handicaps and motor transport was eroding traffic. In 1928 bus operators were licensed to pick up passengers in the town – and the railway closed the following year. When the lines were taken up for scrap to aid the war effort, in 1941, it was the end of any hopes for its revival.

1. *Southwold Railway - crossing the swing bridge over the Blyth. Southwold Museum*

2. *Southwold Railway keys to points and swing bridge. Southwold Museum*

3. *Third class carriage, Southwold Railway. Southwold Museum*

The Belle Steamships

By 1897, in response to growing demand from holidaymakers, the Belle Steamer Company started regular paddle steamer services from the Thames at London Bridge, up the coast to Great Yarmouth. The journey took eleven hours, food and drink were served and you could choose between first and second-class cabins.

Landing at Southwold presented a problem since there was no pier - the steamers hove to offshore and passengers were brought ashore by rowing boat. But Belle was soon taken over by the Coast Development Co., which built a pier in 1900 as part of its ambitious plans to develop Southwold as a resort. From then onwards this was the berth for the steamers - including the 'Southwold Belle', the biggest in a fleet of seven vessels.

In their heyday the steamers brought hundreds of visitors to the town, with daily arrivals from Great Yarmouth and London, but this was a short-lived venture – doomed like the Southwold Railway by the advent of motor transport. In 1910 the Southwold Belle was sold to a French company, and the outbreak of World War One saw the remaining vessels requisitioned and put into service as minesweepers. There was an attempt to revive the service after the war, but the last call to Southwold was made in 1928. In recent years there have been a few nostalgic visits by surviving paddle steamers, lovingly restored.

The Ferry to Walberswick

As with every other means of transport to Southwold, there were attempts from the end of the nineteenth century to modernise the ferry across the river to Walberswick. In 1885 the River Blythe Ferry Company installed a manually driven, chain-link pontoon, to which they soon fitted a steam engine, at a cost of £111. In 1927 a larger, steam-driven pontoon was introduced, capable of carrying vehicles and animals – including on at least one occasion a circus, complete with elephant. But the ferry was discontinued in 1942, and the pontoon was eventually cut up for scrap.

A ferry service was revived after the war, using a simple rowing boat, and so it remains. When you pay Dani Church to row you across the river, you are travelling as our ancestors did eight hundred years ago. It has gone full circle.

1. *A Rolls Royce crosses the river, c.1930.
   Southwold Museum*

2. *The old ferry prior to 1885. Southwold Museum*

The Grand Hotel (built by Coast Development Co) and bathing machines. Southwold Museum

Building the Twentieth Century Town
The Coast Development Company

In the early years of the twentieth century, the town almost doubled in size. The impetus for this astonishing growth was the Coast Development Company, which in 1888 approached the Corporation with a proposal to transform Southwold into a major resort – complete with a Pier, where their own Belle Steamers could unload visitors to Southwold. The land they wished to develop was the Town Farm and brickworks, north of the church - part of William Godell's bequest in the sixteenth century.

Southwold Corporation agreed to sell the Farm for £8,000 and the Development Company started work. They constructed an electricity generating station, installed sewers, laid out Pier Avenue, Cautley Road, Marlborough Road, Field Stile Road and Hotson Road and built three new hotels - the seventy-bedroom Grand on the seafront, the Station Hotel (now the Blyth) and the Randolph in Reydon. But when they offered serviced plots for sale, the take-up was slow, and few houses were built. In 1906 the Company was wound up.

The proceeds from the sale of the Town Farm enabled the Corporation to construct a new cottage hospital on Field Stile Road, which was opened in 1903, and to build Council houses for workmen in St Edmunds Road - sixteen in 1905 and twelve more in 1913. Southwold was amongst the first councils in the country to provide low cost rented accommodation.

These good works were insufficient to placate local opinion, judging by an anonymous notice preserved by a former Town Clerk. 'LOST between the months of September 1888 and August 1900 a quaint little fishing village answering to the name of Southwold, age unknown, colour blue and brown with green spots. Clothed simply and prettily. When last seen was being chased by the East Coast Development Co. Anyone giving advice or information which will lead to its recovery will receive the hearty thanks of its friends and well wishers.'

Revival of the Fishing Industry

Conditions at the river mouth remained a constant problem throughout the nineteenth century, with the entrance frequently blocked by sandbars. In 1839 the town sold its farm at Walpole to raise money to pay for keeping the river open, but trade dwindled and the harbour finally closed in 1884.

An upsurge in the herring fishing industry at the end of the nineteenth century prompted the Corporation to renewed action. Funds were raised, Government financial assistance given and the Southwold Harbour Co established in 1898.

The harbour was leased to the Company, which spent £45,000 on improvements, including sea walls, piers and a fish market -

the octagonal 'Kipperdrome', on the site of today's caravan park.

Between 1907 and 1909, congestion in Lowestoft and Yarmouth harbours caused a dramatic increase in the number of Scottish trawlers landing their catch at Southwold, from under 300 to 761 - and longshore fishing prospered in parallel with drifting, with 120 boats trawling and shrimping off Southwold beach. Thousands of barrels of herring were exported each season to Germany, after being gutted and packed in brine by the famous Scottish fisher girls, who followed the fleet south. The girls stayed for the season in town or went over to Walberswick on the ferry, where they would stroll together - knitting and smoking - and provoking the local lads. Many took a fancy to them, but few could understand their accent (a mutual problem) and the aroma of herring clung to their clothes. Some landladies are even said to have lined the walls of their rooms with newspaper, as protection from fish oil.

It was a short-lived boom. Improved facilities at Lowestoft lured the trawlers back to a port with better connections, and the onset of the first World War coincided with a sharp decline in the herring catches. The enterprise failed and in 1931 the Corporation bought back the lease on the Harbour.

Arts & Crafts

To help fishermen provide for their families in the winter, a local resident, Arthur Flowers, had the idea of setting up wood-working classes, taught by an award-winning craftsman, George Voisey.

The classes began in 1892 and proved so popular that within a year there were 43 members – men, women and children. They brought their own wood and tools and learnt to make furniture, picture frames and all manner of carved items - some of which they submitted to an exhibition at the Albert Hall, where they fetched £44.

Flowers then paid for dedicated premises - The Southwold School of Industrial Art - a classic Arts and Crafts building which opened in Park Lane, in 1894.
The venture flourished and the pupils continued to win prizes and commissions at London shows, until the outbreak of War in 1914. Then the School closed, but the woodcarving tradition survived. The Mayor's chair was carved in 1926 by William Bennett - a former pupil - and an oak settle carved by Bennett is in daily use at the Crown. The School itself is now a private house, but its façade has survived almost unchanged.

Walberswick, meanwhile, was becoming famous as an artists' colony, attracting the likes of Philip Wilson Steer and Charles Rennie Mackintosh. Then Joseph Southall found inspiration on Southwold beach – and this was the beginning of an unexpectedly diverse artistic tradition, including Stanley Spencer in the 1930s and more recently the great colourist Margaret Mellis, whose driftwood constructions briefly inspired Damien Hirst.

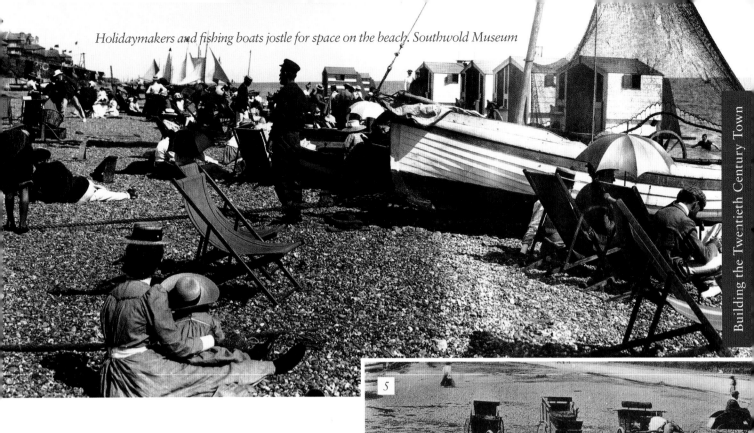

Holidaymakers and fishing boats jostle for space on the beach. Southwold Museum

5

Waiting for Orders, Southwold

Seaside Holidays in the 1900s.

Southwold beach in the summer season was crowded with boats and bathing machines, fishermen and visitors. You could take a jaunt in a goat cart, enjoy a salt-water shower in the Bath Rooms on Ferry Road, go to the circus, have your fortune told at Trinity Fair or compete in the Model Yacht Regatta. Those of a more active disposition could join the Southwold Sailing Club, play golf, tennis, bowls or badminton, hire a cycle or take a steamer trip to Felixstowe or Walton. Or you could cheer on the competitors at the annual sports meeting on the Common, which included a tug-o-war, at which the Brewery team excelled. In the evening there was the Cinema, or concert parties in the Pier Pavilion. When deciding where to stay, the choice ranged from the splendours of the Grand Hotel (special rates for

servants and chauffeurs) to boarding at one of the numerous private houses that took in summer visitors.

Seaside holidays at Southwold had a cheerful, innocent air, perfectly captured in the postcards of Reg Carter.

6

Look inside for some pretty bits of SOUTHWOLD.

4

1. The 'Kipperdrome' and trawlers at Southwold Harbour c.1908. Southwold Museum

2. Scottish girls packing herring. Southwold Museum

3. Woodworking class at the Southwold School of Industrial Art. Southwold Museum

4. Postcard by Reg Carter. Southwold Museum

5. Goat carts. Southwold Museum

6. Tom Benham and his yacht 'Moab', from cartoon of members of the Southwold Sailing Club c.1900. Swan Hotel, Southwold

World War I
Belgian Refugees

The holidaymakers disappeared when Britain declared war on Germany in August 1914. Within weeks, recruits mustered in the Market Place and marched with the band and crowds to the railway station. A troop of the Lincolnshire Yeomanry set up camp on the Common and hundreds of Belgian refugees arrived by boat across the sea.

Eighty miles from the Allied front, Southwold was at war. On still nights residents could hear the dull boom of the guns in Flanders, and the fear of German invasion persisted until the end.

Troops in the Town

In 1915 the Army and the Town Council introduced tough regulations about lights. Special constables used St Edmund's Church tower as an observation post, pinpointing offenders. Many Southwold people, as well as soldiers, were prosecuted and fined.

Army units came and went as the carnage continued in Flanders. The Yeomanry were replaced by the Duke of Westminster units, with 15 armoured cars parked in the High Street. In March the Royal Sussex cyclists (a bicycle mounted regiment) arrived, 670 strong. They were replaced by the Bedfonts, who mounted guard in the Market Place at 6.30pm, and cheered up the town with a brass band. Next came the Montgomery Yeomanry with 500 horses, many of which were stabled on the Common along Rope Walk. Tons of shingle were put down – bedevilling allotment holders there to this very day.

1. *Belgian refugees being fed in Constitution Hall Southwold Museum*

2. *Armoured cars in the High Street. Southwold Museum*

3. *A mine on Walberswick Beach. Southwold Museum*

Zeppelin over Southwold. Southwold Museum

Zeppelins over Southwold

April 1915 saw the first air raid. Zeppelin L6 passed over the town shortly before midnight and followed the railway line to Halesworth, before dropping bombs and incendiaries at Henham Hall – occupied by war wounded looked after by the Southwold Red Cross – and then more bombs at Reydon. One incendiary fell on the railway station, landing in a coal truck. A local fisherman was said to have looked out of his bedroom window when he heard the weird burr of the airship, and decided it was so close that he could throw a stick at it. His wife said: 'For God's sake don't do that. Think of the children.'

1917 saw a brief bombardment of the town by German naval vessels, including a submarine. 68 shells were fired, many of which fell on the marshes but three hit buildings, including the Police Station. Later that year a Zeppelin was shot down, crashing in flames at Theberton.

Peace

The town bristled with pillboxes, barbed wire and gun emplacements, but was defenceless in the last weeks of the war against the pandemic of Spanish flu, which killed some 200,000 people in Britain. Several died in Southwold, including the landlord of the Red Lion.

On 11 November 1918, the guns fell silent. The Mayor, Mr Edgar Pipe, ordered the church bells to ring and read the official telegram from the balcony of the Swan.
There was a short thanksgiving service in St Edmund's Church.

The memorial on Bartholomew Green bears the names of 51 men and one woman killed during the war.

Southwold beach in the 1930s. Southwold Museum

Between the Wars
Beach Huts, Beauty Queens and George Orwell

Southwold between the wars seemed determined to stop the clock. A tourist guide to the town, printed in 1932, extolled its simple seaside pleasures but made no concessions to the mass market. 'Beyond its natural beauties little is done to attract the recognised tripper.' Beach huts (then known as 'beach bungalows') first appeared on the Promenade in 1920s and became an established feature of summer life, but in most other respects little had changed since pre-war days. The annual election of the Beauty Queen was an elaborate pageant of the most proper sort, with not a swimsuit in sight.

It is hardly surprising that Eric Blair (later famous as George Orwell) felt stifled when he returned to his parents' home in Southwold in 1929. He fell in love with a gym teacher at St Felix Girls School, was turned down when he proposed marriage, and longed to get away.
But after he left, Orwell still had his suits made by Denny of Southwold.

The Brewery Expands

One of those with whom Eric Blair was on somewhat frosty nodding terms was Pierse Loftus, Chairman of Adnams, who was elected MP for Lowestoft in 1934.

Irish in origin, P C Loftus had trained as a brewer in Copenhagen and Munich and worked in South Africa, before arriving in Southwold in 1902, at the age of twenty four.

With financial assistance from his stepfather, he acquired a stake in Adnams and immediately set about re-organising the business. Times were hard – the Company paid no dividend until after the First World War - but P C kept everyone on their toes and Adnams expanded, taking over the smaller firms of C J Fisher of Eye in 1903, Rope of Orford in 1922 and Flintham Hall of Aldeburgh in 1924.

The Sole Bay Brewery was re-equipped, the Swan Hotel enlarged and the reputation of Adnams beers began to grow, as prizes were won in international competitions. A fleet of motor vehicles replaced the lumbering Foden steamer, and distribution increased to pubs within about thirty miles of Southwold.
Things were looking up.

1. *Miss Doy crowned Beauty Queen 1937. Southwold Museum*

2. *Adnams enamel signs, prior to 1st World War*

3. *Adnams W&G motor lorry, later converted to Southwold Fire engine. Adnams Archive*

4. *Southwold Fireman's helmet, dented by falling beam 1920s. Southwold Museum*

5. *International Star of Excellence awarded to Adnams 1953. Adnams Archive*

Trinity Fair

A wonderful panorama of Trinity Fair in 1933, painted
by a London solicitor and part-time artist, Mr J Dorman
Turner, is preserved at the Swan. South Green is a
colourful riot of showmen's waggons, stalls and rides -
Bert Stocks Galloping Horses & Cockerels, the Dodgems
('You bring the girl, we've got the car'), Sonya and Olga's
Daring Midnight Cabaret, the Mysterious Maydora
('She's lovely at making Whoopee'). Madame Amiel,
the Great East Anglian Palmist, who pitched her booth
beside Professor Leo – Clairvoyance, Crystal Gazing,
Phrenologist & Medical Adviser. There were coconut
shies, shooting galleries and a chance to smash china.

This anarchic, raucous affair, in the genteel heart of
Southwold, was opened then, as it still is every year,
by the Mayor and Corporation in all their finery, taking
a ride on the merry go round.

1. *Opening of Trinity Fair 1935. Southwold Museum*

2. *Duke of York (later George VI) on Southwold beach
   c.1936. Southwold Museum*

3. *King George VI rowed ashore 1938.
   Southwold Museum*

Trinity Fair scroll 1933 (detail). Swan Hotel, Southwold

2

3

The Duke of York's Camps

In the 1920s the Duke of York (later King George VI) instigated his annual summer camps, inviting hundreds of boys between the ages of 17 and 19, from all walks of life and all parts of the country, to enjoy to a week under canvas – with the motto 'Abandon rank all ye who enter here.' When the camps outgrew their original location the Town Council made an offer of the Common, which was immediately accepted. The first camp at Southwold took place in August 1931.

The boys arrived by train at Halesworth, were transported in a fleet of buses to Southwold and unloaded at a large and immaculate encampment, stretching from the edge of the town to the water tower. They slept on straw mattresses but were catered for in astonishing style, with chefs from Harrods and the Savoy. Their days were full of activities, including morning and evening prayers and the obligatory dip in the sea, for which they were

rewarded with biscuits. For twenty-four hours the Duke would stay with them, arriving and leaving without ceremony and sharing in the games and entertainments.

Despite his request for informality, dignitaries of one sort or another felt it their duty to make an appearance, often overdressed. The Duke, by contrast, invariably wore shorts, sweater and plimsolls, and was more at ease than on most official occasions. This was even true when he came as King George VI to the last camp, in 1938. He arrived by Royal Yacht but was rowed ashore in a small fishing boat, seeming thoroughly to enjoy himself.

Just over a year later, the King was struggling to overcome his stammer as he made the most important speech of his life, to a nation at war.

Churchill signs the Swan Hotel register on visit to Southwold 21 June 1940. Swan Hotel, Southwold

World War II
On the Front Line

When Britain went to war with Germany for the second time in 25 years, on 3 September 1939, Southwold was surprisingly well prepared. Local territorial soldiers had been mobilised in the early autumn of 1938 and trenches dug in various parts of the town. Air Raid wardens, Red Cross and Ambulance parties, road repair gangs, decontamination and rescue services, local firemen and special constables were trained.

Within days of the outbreak of war, gas masks were supplied to townsfolk and fifteen concrete air-raid shelters built. The cannons on Gun Hill were buried to avoid giving the Germans any excuse to shell or bomb the unfortified town. Even beach huts played their part and were scattered over The Common to deter enemy gliders. The Grand and other hotels, the school and empty buildings were taken over by the War Office for troops.

Dozens of children arrived, evacuees from London, clutching small suitcases and with identification labels attached to their overcoats - but the evacuation of Dunkirk and the prospect of a German invasion meant that Southwold was suddenly a frontline town. Women, children and the elderly left for other parts of the country as the population was reduced to about 800 and the town closed to holidaymakers.

Barbed wire covered the beach and hundreds of mines were laid along the shoreline. Engineers blew a hole in the pier in case the Germans landed on the end of it. Road signs were removed. Sticky-tape criss-crossed the windows of every building. To defend the town against naval attacks two six-inch guns were installed in the front garden of a seafront villa.

Air Raids

The greatest danger to Southwold was from low-flying aircraft, which swept in over the sea below radar cover. The first bombs hit the town on 20 August 1940, causing little damage, but the German Focke-Wulfs returned the next afternoon, dropping 1,000lb bombs, which demolished three houses in Lorne Road and damaged 100 houses and shops. The following May during a night raid, bombs damaged houses on Barnaby Green, York Road and the High Street, and later that month more than 500 incendiary bombs were dropped. One hit St Edmund's Hall, which was burnt out.

The air raids were stepped up in 1943. In February a lone German bomber dropped a bomb near houses in Pier Avenue destroying one of them, partially demolishing seven others and damaging a further twelve, though no one was killed. May saw the worst raid of the war. Seven fighter-bombers targeting Lowestoft spotted barrage balloons over the port, turned south and flew at 100 feet above Southwold. One bomb destroyed a building in the grounds of St Felix School. Four more hit the town, blowing out the windows of St Edmund's Church and destroying nearby houses in Hollyhock Square, killing six people. The Marlborough and Dunwich Hotels were also hit.

There were few other raids until February 1944 when more than 1000 incendiary bombs were dropped on the Common where anti-aircraft guns were placed. In October the flying bombs (known as 'Doodle Bugs') began passing over Southwold, on their way to London. The gunners hit one of them, which exploded, damaging more than 600 buildings.

Peace Returns

Troops stationed here to deter an invasion departed, much of the barbed wire along the beach, and all of the mines, were removed. Those evacuated returned and the battered and shabby town gradually revived. Street parties were held to mark the end of the war.

119 bombs and 2,689 incendiaries fell on Southwold during the war. Thirteen civilians were killed and 49 injured. More than 2,000 properties were damaged and 77 totally destroyed. The names of 20 servicemen who died in action were added to those on the war memorial.

1. *Southwold Town Hall protected from air raids. Southwold Museum*

2. *Trenches on Southwold cliff top. Southwold Museum*

3. *Troops exercising near Southwold. Southwold Museum*

4. *Bomb damage to the church May 1943. Southwold Museum*

1953 – Disaster and Celebrations

The Great Flood

On the night of 31 January 1953, gale-force northerly winds sent a massive surge of water funnelling round from Scotland into the North Sea. As the sea narrowed between the bulge of East Anglia and the coast of Holland, the surge combined with an unusually high spring tide, overwhelming sea defences in both countries. It was one of the worst floods ever to hit England, in which 358 people lost their lives.

Southwold did not escape. The sea rushed in with extraordinary force over Ferry Road, sweeping away houses, caravans, people and animals. The pub and cottages at Blackshore were flooded to the first floor and the water continued far inland, submerging low-lying bungalows at Wolsey Bridge and Blythburgh. It was a night of drama, heroic rescues and tragedy, in which five people died. But it also provoked the old wartime spirit of 'Keep Calm and Carry On'. As the storm subsided, a rowing boat could be seen pulling across the Town Marshes, laden with beer to replenish the Harbour Inn.

The Coronation

Southwold celebrated the Coronation of Elizabeth II as the dawn of a new era. Magnificent, three-dimensional heraldic beasts – the Lion and the Unicorn - marked the entrance to the High Street, which was lined with brightly coloured poles, from which fluttering drapes looped high above the middle of the road, where they miraculously supported a series of golden crowns, all the way down to the Market Place. Everything was designed and made by the Decorations Sub Committee, with a determination to outdo anywhere else for miles around – as they brilliantly did.

The week long programme of events included church services, the opening of Trinity Fair, bonfires, balls and a carnival – and a children's tea party, with slices of Coronation Cake (baked in the shape of Buckingham Palace), and the presentation of Coronation mugs. All of which was presided over by the town's redoubtable Mayor, Fanny Foster.

4

Christmas

Buoyed by success, Southwold finished the year with style. The High Street was lined with coloured lanterns and fir trees in beer barrels, and a large 'Alpine Chalet' was built round the pump in the Market place, crowned by a life-size Father Christmas in a sleigh drawn by reindeer. Night after night until Christmas Eve there were carols and choirs, bands and hand-bells - as visitors and locals packed the town.

The austerity of the post-war years was behind them. There was hope for the future.

3

1. *The storm batters the pier on night of 31 June 1953. Painting by Frank Forward. Southwold Museum*

2. *The Harbour Inn is resupplied with beer, 1 Feb 1953. Adnams archive*

3. *Christmas 'chalet' in Marketplace 1953. Southwold Museum*

Battling the Predators
Fanny Foster

The diminutive figure of Fanny Foster - three times Mayor of Southwold - personified the town's determination to protect its unique character when threatened by unsympathetic developers. This astonishing woman – a Cambridge graduate, self-taught photographer, fluent in Serb-Croat – lived in Park Lane for most of her life and was deeply involved in Southwold's affairs. She fought fiercely for its preservation, often in alliance with Nicholas Loftus, who combined his role as Managing Director of Adnams with the Chairmanship of the County Planning Committee. Between them they defeated many a destructive scheme to 'modernize' the town. Once, when challenged by a journalist who asked what Southwold thought of some project that she opposed, Fanny memorably declared, 'I am Southwold.' She was right – and much loved for it.

1. *Decimalisation comes to Southwold 1970.*
    Southwold Museum

2. *Mr Marshall the baker and his Coronation Cake 1953.*
    Southwold Museum

Unveiling of new Town Sign 1951 - designed by Clifford Russel (in wheelchair). The Mayor, Town Mace-bearer, Fanny Roster (in hat with dark ribbon), Nicholas Loftus and his father P.C. Loftus. Southwold Museum

The Brewery Under Threat

Two factors threatened the survival of Adnams in the 1950s and 60s. One was the massive process of consolidation in the brewing industry, with companies large and small being taken over. The other was the development of keg beer – filtered, pasteurised, bland and trouble free.

ADNAMS & CO LTD

RECOMMENDED

PUBLIC BAR PRICES

DRAUGHT BEERS
	Per Pint		Per ½ Pint	
Mild Ale (XXX)	2/2	11p	1/1	5½p
Best Bitter	2/5	12p	1/3	6p
Strong Ale (XXXX)	2/7	13p	1/4	6½p

BOTTLED BEERS
	Per Small Bottle		Per Nip	
Nut Brown Ale	1/3	6p		
Pale Ale	1/4	6½p		
Nourishing Stout	1/5	7p		
Fisherman (Strong Ale)	1/6	7½p	1/3	6p
Tally Ho (Barley Wine)			1/9	9p

ADNAMS & CO LTD
SOLE BAY BREWERY
SOUTHWOLD

30th NOVEMBER, 1970

At a time when traditional cask beer varied wildly in quality and was often poorly served, keg was seen as the answer by publicans across the country. Within a few years many of East Anglia's breweries had been swallowed up and their beers were replaced by Watneys Red Barrel.

Adnams was determined to survive, its spirit of independence echoing that of the town. Numerous offers of takeover were refused and a growing band of enthusiasts proclaimed their loyalty to Adnams beer. The Company suffered a severe blow when Nicholas Loftus was killed in a car accident in 1963, but members of the third generation of the Adnams and Loftus families joined the business and their arrival coincided with the revival of 'real ale', encouraged by CAMRA. Demand increased, additional capacity was installed, the future seemed increasingly secure.

Survival of the Shopkeepers

Southwold's isolation at the end of a road to the sea meant that it retained an astonishing range of independent shops. Denny & Son boasted that they were 'Tailors of Southwold and Saville Row' – in that order. Mr Baggott the butcher frequently served as Town Mayor. George Bumstead the grocer sold bacon and cheese and coffee and all manner of tins and packets – as well as being Curator of Southwold Museum. Arthur Swan the fishmonger told scandalous tales of his days as cook on a millionaire's yacht, and was famous for his cold-smoked mackerel. Marshalls the bakers had queues for their heart-stopping Butter Buns, made to a secret recipe. Reggie Mumford the ironmonger brought the house down at the annual variety show in St Edmund's Hall, with his rendition of 'I am the fairy on the Christmas Tree.' And Penelope Fitzgerald worked at the Sole Bay Bookshop, which later inspired her first novel.

Supermarkets and chain stores were unheard of.

1

Into the Twenty First Century

Southwold has lost its status as a self-governing borough and the resident population has declined to less than a thousand, as ever more houses are acquired as holiday homes. But in many essential ways the town has preserved its character. The numerous greens and hidden alleys, the space of its wonderful Common and the towers of Lighthouse and Church give pleasure to all who live there - and the texture of local life has a satisfying diversity. Fishermen still sell their catch from black-tarred huts at the harbour - which is a delightfully messy place, where boat repairers jostle with tourists, yachtsmen and the lifeboat station. The Pier has recently been re-built and the Southwold beach huts preserve the feel of a classic seaside holiday. There are too many clothes shops, but this is a good place to forage for food and drink, and supports a wide range of pubs and restaurants.

At the heart of Southwold's commercial life is Adnams Brewery – nationally renowned and locally loved. The business has expanded considerably, moving its most intrusive activities out of town to a new, environmentally friendly distribution centre nearby, but continues to brew in Southwold. Gleaming, energy efficient equipment is hidden behind the nineteenth century façade of the Sole Bay Brewery, to which a small, high quality distillery has recently been added.

There is a flourishing season of Summer Theatre, an annual autumn Literacy Festival, Winter Lectures orgainsed by the Museum and frequent concerts in the church.

All these elements guard something of Southwold's history. Most hold hope for the future.

2

1. *Adnams Distillery Southwold. Image flikr - oosp*

2. *Southwold Pier. Image Simon Hazelgrove.*

In Memory of Alan Bottomley

As with all historians of Southwold, I am indebted to my predecessors – beginning with Thomas Gardner, Salt Tax Officer and local antiquarian, who published his great work in 1754. The nineteenth century saw a verbose but invaluable book by the town's second Mayor, Robert Wake, and the compilation of an astonishing mixture of scrapbooks and diaries by the auctioneer and schoolmaster James Maggs. A hundred and fifty years later another schoolmaster, Alan Bottomley, edited Maggs's diaries for publication and wrote his own *Short History of Southwold*, distilling his notes for what was intended to be a much larger work, unfortunately never completed.

It was Bottomley - known to everyone as Bill - who introduced me to the treasure trove of seventeenth and eighteenth century records that were then, quite casually, stored in cardboard boxes in Southwold Town Hall.

Bill helped me decipher the unfamiliar writing, shared his expertise with unfailing generosity and attempted to curb my wilder flights of speculation. His death deprived us of the definitive history of Southwold.

This brief work is dedicated to his memory.

I am also happy to acknowledge my debt to fellow members of the Southwold Museum & Historical Society, on whose researches I have drawn and without whose help this book could not have been compiled. They include John & Margaret Child, Diana Dixon, Hilary Huckstep, Jenny Hursell, David & Sheila de Kretser, the late Rachel Lawrence, David Lee, John Miller, Paul Scriven, Barry Tolfree and Cynthia Wade. Many of the illustrations were specially commissioned from the photographer, Stephen Wolfenden, who gave generously of his time. This book has been designed by Glen Cone of Spring. To all of them, and to the numerous volunteers who keep the Museum running, many thanks.

Simon Loftus
President, Southwold Museum & Historical Society April 2012.

ISBN 978-0-9572261-0-4

Published by Southwold Museum, 9-11 Victoria Street, Southwold, Suffolk IP18 6HZ
www.southwoldmuseum.org

An illustrated history of
SOUTHWOLD

Simon Loftus

A SOUTHWOLD MUSEUM PUBLICATION